Stay Magic!
xo, Andi Stein

Copyright © 2020 Andrea Stein.

All rights reserved. This book or parts thereof may not be reproduced in any form, stored in any retrieval system, or transmitted in any form by any means—electronic, mechanical, photocopy, recording, or otherwise—without prior written permission of the publisher, except as provided by United States of America copyright law. For permission requests, write to the publisher at moondustpresspub@gmail.com.

ISBN:978-1-7341081-0-1 (Hardcover)
ISBN:978-1-7341081-1-8 (E-Book)

Library of Congress Control Number:2019919766

Names, characters, places and events are products of the author's imagination, and any resemblance to actual events or places or persons, living or dead, is entirely coincidental.

First printing edition 2020.

Moon Dust Press
Austin, Texas
United States of America
www.moondustpress.com

To Luna, for everything. -A.S.

For Junie Moon, my magic girl. -C.M.

She learns about the ancient craft through

art,

and earth,

and **play**.

"There are many types of witches," says her mother, rightly so.

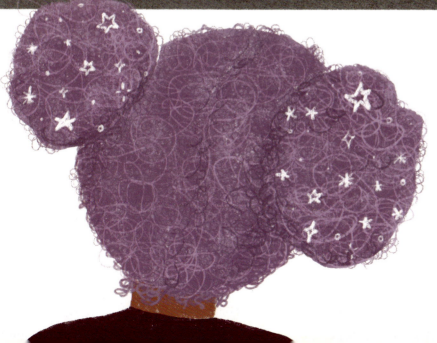

But Brina doesn't know which way her witchy heart will go...

Maybe she'd be a green witch and that was quite a thought, concocting herbal remedies when magic spells are sought.

Or maybe yet a **kitchen witch**, working away at home,

that little spark of magic
always there and free to roam.

Perhaps training as a hedge witch would turn out to be her style.

Lost in solitary spell work,
and learning all the while.

Her mind wandered to Wicca.
Now that could be the one!
Minding the law of threefold,
doing good, and harming none.

So many different pantheons.
Oh, how was one to choose?

Norse, Egyptian, Ancient Greek.

She really couldn't lose!

Another thing that Brina knew was witches needed tools to channel all their power through while making their own rules.

Of course, a witch can always find a partner in a wand.

Tarot, runes, and tea leaves
will all help her see beyond.

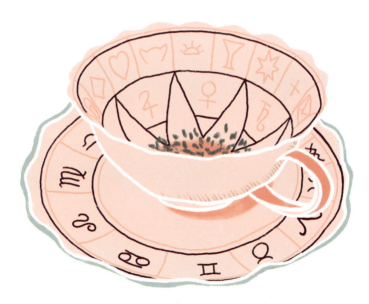

Quartz, Jasper, Amethyst, Aventurine, and Celestite.

Crystals resonate within and let her see the light.

The altar in her home is a very special place.
Candles, bells, and mystic things adorn this sacred space.

"So which witch should I be?" she thought while standing in her room.

Then at that same moment she caught sight of mom's old broom.

She lay back in the damp grass to track phases of the moon,
and has a feeling something big is coming her way soon.

it's only a matter of time before she's up, up, and away.